Rules for Discerning the Spirits

The author, **Rev. Fr. Ludovic-Marie Barrielle**, was a priest renowned for his preservation of traditional spirituality in the face of experimental eastern and occult spiritualities. To accommodate his popularity, Fr. Barrielle joined the Cooperators of Christ the King, a small order of priests whose special charism was preaching the *Spiritual Exercises* of St. Ignatius of Loyola. As retreat masters travelling throughout Europe, the souls of thousands of religous and lay people were to benefit from the Cooperators in general and Fr. Barrielle in particular. At the death of Fr. Vallet, the founder of the Cooperators of Christ the King, Fr. Barrielle was elected Superior General of the Order. He resigned in 1971 to become Spiritual Director at the International Seminary of St. Pius X in Switzerland. It is from the best of his many retreat conferences that this book is drawn. In a time when Catholic priests are now no longer as accessible for counsel as in years past, the spiritual wisdom of Fr. Barrielle's legacy is more necessary than ever.

In the *Spiritual Exercises* of St. Ignatius of Loyola

ANGELUS PRESS
2915 Forest Avenue, Kansas City, Missouri 64109

ANGELUS PRESS
2915 FOREST AVENUE
KANSAS CITY, MISSOURI 64109
PHONE (816) 753-3150
FAX (816) 753-3557
ORDER LINE 1-800-966-7337
www.angeluspress.org

ISBN 978-0-935942-77-3
Fifth Printing—July 2007

Printed in the United States of America

RULES OF THE FIRST WEEK FOR DISCERNING THE SPIRITS

(or ELEMENTARY RULES FOR DISTINGUISHING SPIRITUAL INFLUENCES)

"The life of man is a battle upon earth," said Job. We must expect to fight continually for the whole of our lives. The difficulty is that in these battles, where we defend our souls from the attacks of the devil, one does not see the enemy (just as the eyes of our body do not see the celestial spirits that God sends to aid us). We should remember the scene in the Second Book of Kings (6:15-17): The village in which the prophet Eliseus happened to be was surrounded by chariots of the Syrian king with orders to capture the prophet alive and to bring him to the king; the servant of the king cried out: "Alas, alas, alas, my lord, what shall we do?" And Eliseus replied "Fear not: for there are more with us than with them." And he prayed to the Lord. Yahweh opened the eyes of the servant, and he saw a mountain full of horses and chariots of fire surrounding Eliseus.... We must fight in the same way. We do not see those who attack us, because the devils are pure spirits. But Our Lord has given us His angels, whom we do not see either. These are more numerous and more powerful than the devils.

St. Paul writes in the last chapter of his letter to the Ephesians: "Put you on the armor of God, that you may be able to stand against the deceits of the devil. For our wrestling is not against flesh and blood; but against principalities and powers, against rulers of the world of this darkness, against the spirits of wickedness in the high places. Therefore take unto you the armor of God, that you may be able to resist in the evil day, and stand in all things perfect."

The devil does all in his power to make us believe that he does not exist or to think not of him. It is then that he is able to act with all freedom. This is the reason for all these attempts to deny the existence of the angels that we hear repeated sometimes even in the sacristies: because if there were no angels there would not be any devils, and yet, the angels, both the good and the bad, are found in Holy Scripture from the first chapter to the last.

This, however, is not sufficient for them to believe in the existence of angels and devils. One has to wake up! A Spanish proverb says: "When someone knocks at the door, one does not only hear the knocking, but also, one must realize WHO is knocking."

Many people do not realize the influences that a spirit can have on us.

: Father, I'm down in the dumps!

: No, sir, you are not down in the dumps. That does not exist. You have the devil hovering about you.

: Father, you see the devil everywhere. I'm down in the dumps because the sun is not out today, and when the weather is bad I'm sad, that's all! It has nothing to do with the devil.

: Exactly! Do you not know that the devil uses everything when coming to tempt you? He will use advantageously the bad weather, as a disposition. You just are not aware of the fact that if you are feeling sad, the devil is hovering about you. Beware!

Behold a sad young man. I do not say that he has sinned. I say: "The devil is hovering about him." Attention! How does one know that?... There are rules, brought by the Blessed Virgin Mary to St. Ignatius.

One must above all distinguish well that which is from God, let us say from the Good Spirit and that which comes from the evil spirit. God either acts directly or by the mediation of an angel, a preacher, a good example, etc. Also, when the devil acts, it is either by himself or through one of his henchmen, bad counsel or example, etc. Lastly, there are acts which come from our intelligence and from our will; for these only we are responsible.

How many youngsters are troubled because they have bad thoughts! The fact of having bad thoughts is not a sin. It is the cinema that the devil projects into our sensible faculties, imagination, memory, etc.

: But they are very evil images!

: It is not you that is evil, it is the devil. If you consent and take pleasure in these evil delectations, you sin, because the consent comes from yourself. You are responsible for it. If, on the contrary, you pray and try to drive away the temptations, not only have you not sinned, but you have gained merit. That is yours. The cinema belongs to the devil.

A holy religious, Sister Rajatella, from Barcelona wrote to St. Ignatius in Rome:

: Father, I have evil thoughts!

St. Ignatius responded:

: I do not trouble myself over evil thoughts that the devil sends me and which I do not accept, nor do I pride myself concerning the good thoughts that my good Angel sends me and are not mine.

And the saint continues:

: Both St. Peter and St. Paul also had bad thoughts, but they did not sin.

St. Paul tells us in the twelfth chapter of his second letter to the Corinthians: *"...there was given me a sting of my flesh, an Angel of Satan to buffet me. For which thing thrice I besought the Lord, that it might depart from me."* And God knows how much the Sacred Heart loved St. Paul! What did Our Lord reply to him? *"My grace is sufficient for thee: for power is made perfect in infirmity."* Well, if St. Peter and St. Paul had evil thoughts, we also can have them. The thing is to know how to behave while under temptation. This is the aim of the rules for distinguishing between different spiritual influences.

Behold, thus, the sub-title (no. 313) of the book of the Exercises. It contains within it the only general and grand principle that must be remembered.

313 : **Rules for distinguishing** *(therefore, there will be nuances to be noted)* **between different spiritual influences** *(for example: I have the desire to become a missionary, to change my resolutions, etc. Beware before acting! Is it from God or the devil?)* **so that the good ones may be admitted** *(it should be noted that if one is sure that it comes from God one must not hesitate to do it. The difficulty is to be sure that it*

comes from God; it is, for that matter, more difficult to know if it is of God), **and the evil ones rejected.**

We have there a general rules which is capital. As soon as one knows that it comes from the devil, it must be rejected without any discussion. My master of novices, Fr. Terradas said, "One does not play with the devil." He calls "playing with the devil" the fact of tarrying with a thought that one knows to be not good, and thus, from the devil (while reassuring oneself, with a firm will, not to consent to it). Woe to him who consents to dialogue with the devil (who is much stronger that we). Eve succumbed because she "played" with the devil. After having told her that God had forbidden it, the devil followed up with new reasons. Instead of cutting him short, she started to discuss with him:

: If we eat of it, we will die.

: No, you will not die, you will become like gods, knowing good and evil!

She discussed, and the devil finished by making her fall.

Behold, a married man:

: No, Father, I love my wife too much. It is only to amuse myself. I dream... only a dream... "If I had to leave my wife, such a one would be so good!"... No! No! Father, it's only a joke. Be assured.

: Sir, you are playing with the devil. Even if it should never happen, and we have seen the impossible happen, the devil succeeds in provoking an adulterous desire! What a victory for him!... Even if he manages only to diminish your union... what a defeat for you!

Another example: A novice or a seminarian... dreams of a beautiful blond, one active in Catholic Action... a beautiful home! "We could have a large family, lots of children, be active in Catholic Action... etc."

: Beware! You are playing with the devil!

: But, Father, it is only a distraction. You know I love my vocation!

: Yes, my dear friend, it is a distraction. It is more than that, it is the devil playing with your imagination. If you accept to return to this agreeable dream, your vocation is lost in advance. Do not amuse yourself with such a game!

St. Bernard wrote: *Nemo repente fit pessimus.* "Nobody becomes suddenly bad." We sometimes hear of priests falling, of great, exemplary Christians falling, etc. Know that it has not happened all of a sudden. For a long time, they have played with the devil.

Rules For Distinguishing Between Spiritual Influences Of The First Week.

(Namely, for all sinners both at the beginning and advanced in the ways of the interior life.)

How do I know that an inspiration that I feel comes from God or from the devil? There are rules. These rules differ for those who are living in the state of sin and for those who are making progress in virtue.

FIRST RULE No. 314

314 : *Those who go from mortal sin to mortal sin are usually influenced in this way: the enemy proposes certain illusory delights, causing them to imagine sensual pleasures and enjoyments, the more effectively to keep them under the sway of their vicious and sinful course. The good spirit deals with these same people in the opposite way, working on their consciences in order to induce compunction and remorse.*

So it is, with those who live in mortal sin: the evil spirit reassures the sinner and pushes him further and further into sin. He presents to the sinner more vivid pleasures, and sensible delectation. He represents to him the objects of sin as the greatest happiness, so that he will plunge deeper and deeper into it with all the more security and joy, just as if it were something normal and indispensable: "The whole world is doing it."

The good angel, on the contrary, sends a sting. He stirs one's conscience, this prevents the sinner from being complacent: he uses rational reproaches. He shows him the consequences of sin. The sinner is in the state of damnation. If his car should hit a lamp post or a milestone, he risks passing from his steering wheel to the judgment of God, and hell.

That is clear... indubitable. The devil makes him reject these thoughts that have converted so many souls!

: Do not worry yourself, God is good! Everybody does it. Just take a look around, it is not worth talking to your confessor about it. It doesn't concern him. You will confess it on your death bed. You will always have enough time! You are still young, etc.

If you have a friend that does not believe, do not go and tell him: "You are just great! I am sure that you will be saved. You gave $2000 to charity, you are intelligent, loyal, obliging, etc."

: No! Tell him the truth!

: With all the intelligence that God gave you, you are the most stupid man in town. You are on the way of perdition... You call yourself loyal? My foot! If you were truly loyal, you would go Chabeuil (a retreat house) and make a retreat... You call yourself a benefactor of humanity? You are a public scandal! Children lose their faith just by looking at you; prepare yourself to render terrible accounts to God, Who has laden you with gifts and to Whom you shall render account... etc.

Those who reassure the sinner in his sins also play the game of the devil. I, on the contrary, have known persons who have been saved because they one day encountered a confessor who said to them:

: Since you are not decided to do away with sin, I cannot grant you absolution, we both would be committing a sacrilege... You must convert!

: If I die will I go to hell?

: If you remain in that state of sin, yes, you shall!

: Well, Father, then I shall return!

The person in question made a complete about turn and fulfilled her Easter duties, not on the day of Easter but before Pentecost. She had four children, she ended up with eleven. She was saved by a confessor who played the game of the good angel.

I know a parish that was converted because the parish priest announced at the beginning of Lent that any one missing a Sunday Mass during Lent would be refused absolution for his Easter duties. It was a very Christian village, so they say, where the men fulfilled their Easter duties and came to Mass four times a year, that's all. After this warning, nothing changed. The day of Easter, none of them were able to fulfill their Easter duty. You should have seen the disturbance that it caused in the village! Well... half of them came to fulfill it at Pentecost, and they continue to come to Mass. A good number of the others came back slowly, at the occasion of a mission or because of some sickness.

It is the devil that reassures the sinner in his sins. **BEWARE!**

The good angel gives "rational reproaches." He says clearly who he is, he does not beat around the bush. If you wish to convert someone, do not give him reasons that are beside the point. For example: "Go to Chabeuil because one eats well there." Tell him rather: "If you had to die at this moment, would you be in a fit state to appear before your God? Well then, you unfortunate person, go quickly and make a good retreat! That is indispensable to you and very urgent."

Fr. Roothan said that this first rule can also be applied to those who, without being in the state of mortal sin, are well entrenched in tepidity. For example, those Christians and religious who have decided not to correct their venial sins. The devil reassures one in tepidity, and it is very dangerous for their salvation. The good angel sends him grave warnings. Woe to those who pay no attention! It is in this way that laxity is introduced into many convents and even into Christian families.

SECOND RULE No. 315

How does the evil spirit proceed? How does the good angel behave with those who work courageously at correcting their sins?

The devils, as well as the good angels, are pure spirits. We do not see them. God did not want the devils, our enemies, to come and attack us without us having something like a "rule" by which to detect them. This is why the examination of conscience is so important. *"Vigilate et orate"* said Jesus in the Gospels: *"Watch and pray."* Woe to the Christian that is not on his guard! The devil will do with his soul as he pleases if he is not alert. But to watch is not sufficient... we must also recognize the signs which discern the good angel from the bad one.

St. Ignatius gives us six signs by which to recognize the evil spirit who seeks to tempt those who progress in virtue.

315 : *The contrary prevails with those who are making earnest progress in self-purification, rising from good to better in the service of God, Our Lord. In these cases it is typical of the evil spirit to cause regret and sadness, using fallacious arguments to disturb them and to impede their progress...*

We have thus six characteristics, like six odors, that betray the evil spirit:

1. Sadness.

"A saint sad is a sad saint," said St. Francis de Sales. The devil is eternally sad... he cannot get rid of his sadness. As soon as he comes near you he communicates his sadness without even so much as wanting to do so. This is so much the case, that in the rules for discerning the spirits of the second week, when the devil attempts to tempt a fervent soul, under the appearance of good, one of the signs for recognizing that it is the devil is this sadness that we feel overcoming us. Such is one who, leaving the confessional content, is suddenly struck by sadness. Recognize him who comes near with his sadness! Behold a sad young man: I do not say that he has sinned, but I know that the devil is hovering about him. Beware of these melancholic dreams! One may not realize, but the devil is not far off!

2. Regret.

Fr. Louis Lallamant, the famous Jesuit said: "All conditional propositions that disturb one's soul, come from the devil."

Behold, your wife arrives one Saturday evening:

: Who knows, Francis, if I have made a good confession? Who knows if tomorrow I will be able to go to Communion?

: Why?... Have you intentionally hidden a mortal sin in confession? (And you know that for nothing in the world would she commit a venial sin, let alone a mortal sin.)

: Oh no! But the sacristan was noisy, and the children were making a fuss, Father was sneezing, I was confused. Who knows if I made a good confession?

Reply to her:

: Be assured, you have make a good confession; you can go to Communion in peace.

: How do you know that?

: It's the second rule! It is the devil that is confusing you, and the devil is a liar! If you had made a sacrilegious confession, the devil would have reassured you, while the good angel would tell you why and in what way you would have made a sacrilegious confession. Thus be assured that you have not.

Behold a seminarian who ponders within himself whether or not he has a vocation. These thoughts, in themselves, come from the devil. The good angel would tell him clearly why he does not have a vocation.

3. Impediments.

The devil excels in making the practice of virtue seem too difficult; he blows out of proportion all the difficulties. How many people think that a really Christian life is impossible, that there are insurmountable difficulties in saving oneself, in practicing chastity according to one's state of life, in living as a Christian in marriage! Think of the horror at the thought of not appearing like the rest of the world, which has persuaded so many great Christians to dishonor themselves by impure fashions. How many times has a "panic pregnancy" persuaded an allegedly Catholic woman to commit an infanticide - a crime which cries to heaven for vengeance before God! - to be deprived of that eternal treasure, that unequalled joy for the whole family, which a newly-born baby brings, and which, as we know, provides also the health and happiness of the woman. The devil inflates all the difficulties and at the same time hides that which renders the Christian life easy: flight from occasions of sin, prayer, the sacraments, the profound joys of a Christian family, the eternal bliss, etc.

4. Disturbance.

"All trouble comes from the devil," said St. John Berchmans, including moody temperaments and vivid emotions. Sometimes in the family, there is tension in the air. The wife loses her temper, the children are particularly unbearable, the father is boxing every one's ears. Know that the devil is present! There, he wins every time... Foolish things are said and done, sin is committed more or less gravely, and more or less numerously. *VIGILATE!* Pray! We will explain further on, the means to counterattack the devil's impact. One must warn the children against certain dissipations or feelings of anger or pride which the devil makes use of...

5. Fallacious Reasoning.

Fallacious reasoning is an unmistakable sign of the devil. One must be very skeptical of certain false theories, of certain slogans which engender many sins, and often grave sins against the faith, against justice or charity. For example:

"They can choose their own religion when they grow up."

> : Excuse me! Do you know whether they will live until then? Do they not have a right to know now that they have a Father in heaven?... To know that they have an eternal destiny? Do they not have already a little heart that is capable of practicing virtue?... To love the good God? It is not an act of justice that you are advocating; rather, it is the most horrible and criminal of injustices. **FALSE REASONINGS!**

Also: "Father we will only have one child; that way, we will bring him up better!" Do not be deceived! One does not bring up a single child better than one does twelve. As for me, some of the whippings that I received did not come from my father or my mother, but from brothers and sisters, who also play an important part in an education!

Also: "I did not ask God to come into the world..." or, what comes to the same thing: "I did not ask my parents to bring me into the world." Besides it being foolishness and insuperable pride, one may reply: "At which moment, *sir*, should they have asked your permission? Before your conception?... When you were in the womb of your mother?... when you were sucking your thumb?... or would they have had to wait until you were twenty years old?"

This is assuredly a serious blasphemy against God, the Father of all good. Life is good. Your eternal destiny is a good above all other goods. Consider all the means that God has prepared for you, from all eternity, in order that you save your soul! And your parents, also, did nothing but follow God's plan... And you, being so full of pride, say such things! Do you not make use of all these gifts of God? How dare you not even thank Him? *Ita ut sint inexcusabiles!* (so that they are inexcusable) says St. Paul (Rom. 1:20), talking about those who do not want to say "thank you" to the good God and who, all the same, use His gifts, starting with their morning coffee through to the night. They breathe the good God's air, drink His milk, His wine, His water, they eat His bread, smoke His cigarettes, etc.

6. Discouragement.

Discouragement is the work of the devil. You have begun well... all of a sudden your courage dries up: the devil has passed by. What about the good angel? He provides courage, peace, joy and makes all things easy!

Remember the temptations of St. Augustine! He was in the garden. He was 32 years old, and not even baptized. He had led a dissolute life and became a Manichean. He had a very holy mother who prayed for him during these 32 years. She followed him to Milan, where the emperor appointed him as director of the imperial school. There, he came into contact with St. Ambrose, who had no difficulties in showing the young director (who was very intelligent and loved to hear St. Ambrose speak), that if he wanted to save his soul he would, at all costs, have to become a Christian, to quit his evil ways, to get baptized, etc. He was enrolled as a catechumen and was supposed to be baptized at Easter. Do you honestly believe, from this, that it all went so smoothly? St. Augustine, in his CONFESSIONS (Book 8) tells us how it actually happened. He was in his garden, when all of a sudden he became sad: "You are not stupid; have you reflected enough?" He cried crocodile tears and was even obliged to walk around so that he could breathe. "This is impossible!" All his old friendships flooded his memory: "How could you live without us? Augustine! Oh, dear Augustine! It is impossible!" The temptation was so great that he was on the point of refusing baptism and of sending word to the archbishop:

"Excellency, I am not ready, I underestimated my strength." What a pity! But the good angel does not abandon his own, and while he was walking in the garden, he received an idea: *Quod isti et istae, cur non ego?* "After all, what all these Christians can do... why could I not do it too? Well, just like them, I will flee from the occasions of sin, I will pray; and if I fall, I will go to confession; I will go to Communion... how fortunate I am!" This thought gave him peace and joy: "For Easter I will be like my mother!"

Note well, in the first part, the six signs of the devil: **sadness, regret, impediments, disturbance, false reasonings, discouragement.** Do you see that it was not by chance, nor by his own strength, that St. Augustine kept his resolution? He kept it only because the good angel intervened.

315 : (continued) *...on the other hand, the role of the good angel is to provide courage and strength, to console and inspire, to move to tears, all in a spirit of peace. Everything is made easy, all obstacles are removed, to enable the soul to continue in virtue.*

THIRD RULE No. 316

Concerning Spiritual Consolation and Desolation.

The aim is to know what one must do when the devil is present. St. Ignatius will show us. Before proceeding to indicate how we must behave in the face of an approaching trial or temptation of the devil, he, as a good scholastic, will define the terms that will be used. The devil has often been victorious over generous souls only because of false definitions of spiritual consolation and desolation.

Many Christians confuse consolation with progress in the spiritual life and desolation with regression. These are very different things.

Do not imagine that you are more holy because you feel spiritual consolations (e.g. after Communion, a heart filled with good feelings). Do not become discouraged and believe that you are diminishing in holiness because you have temptations, no matter how evil they are.

How many retreatants have experienced a deep sorrow for their sins on their first retreat and tell us on their second one: "Father, I have messed up my retreat! I am dry... I cannot inflame myself with love." I have known good and generous retreatants who have been shaken during a retreat, even to the point where they asked themselves if they were not in the process of losing the Faith.

This is precisely a retreat where God wants them to get out of the ordinary ways and to progress through the high mystical paths. Pay, then, close attention to the definitions of St. Ignatius.

316 : **ON SPIRITUAL CONSOLATION:** *This is the name I give to any interior movement experienced by the soul, causing it to glow with love for its Creator and Lord, the effect of which is that it can no longer love any earthly creature in itself, but only in the Creator of them all. The name also applies to the shedding of tears leading to love of God, either out of sorrow for sin or for the sufferings of Christ our Lord, or for other reasons directly concerned with His service and praise. Lastly, comfort is the name given to any growth in faith, hope or charity, or to any inward joy which summons or draws a man to the things of the next world, to the saving of his own soul, bringing the soul to peace and tranquility in its Creator and Lord.*

You see them: sorrowing for their sins, sorrowing for the passion of Jesus: he calls it spiritual consolation, because it causes sweet tears. Do not conclude that it makes you more holy. If on the other hand, despite your supplications, you remain dry as a log while wanting to cry for your sins, do not think that your meditation is a failure. How many then become discouraged! Rodriguez tells us of a holy religious who, as soon as he started to meditate, found himself as dry as a log and did not even manage to say a single word to Our Lord. He would ceaselessly repeat: "I am a beast... I am a beast.... " Do not believe that he wasted his time, any more than the poor publican in the Gospel who did not dare to lift his eyes to Heaven while striking his breast and saying: "Lord, have mercy on me, a poor sinner! Have mercy on me! etc."

FOURTH RULE No. 317

317 : **ON SPIRITUAL DESOLATION:** *This is the name that I give to*

whatever is opposite to the foregoing; darkness of soul, disquiet of mind, an attraction to what is coarse and earthly, all restlessness proceeding from different temptations and disturbances, such as the temptation tending to destroy Faith, Hope and Charity; the condition in which the soul finds itself listless, apathetic, melancholy, like one cut off from his Creator and Lord. Inasmuch as comfort and distress are opposed, the thoughts that spring from the former are contrary to those springing from the latter.

Pardon the childish expression: "In times of consolation God gives us sugar. In times of desolation, He gives us a steak as tough as leather." Do not believe that in the first case you are holier and that in the second case that you are more evil... How many people become discouraged because they are bombarded with the most vile and shameful temptations. We will see later how to react. Far from being a sign of falling back, it is, rather, if the correct means are taken, a grace to help us progress in holiness. St. Jeanne de Chantal remained many years prey to terrible temptations. She did not feel like praying. When she did pray, she felt a terrible disgust; she wanted to leave her convent and return to the world in order to live a lax life, worldly and dissolute. She wondered whether she still had the Faith.

Perhaps you will think that she was going backwards along the way of sanctification? On the contrary, it is during these years that she made the most progress in virtue and obtained a generosity and constancy that she would never have reached if the good God had never allowed these trials.

Fr. Vallet said to us: "There are many ways of learning how to box:

1. Some train by punching their pillow. In doing that, only meagre results will be made.
2. Others train with a punching ball. That makes for greater progress (if not, one risks getting the ball in one's face).
3. If one wants to become a proficient boxer, one must train with a champion. In the beginning you will be bruised, but soon you, too, will become a master.

"Thus," added Fr. Vallet, "God permits the devil to tempt us, in order to help us advance rapidly in holiness."

"Because you were agreeable to God, it is necessary that you be tried by temptation," said the Archangel Raphael to Tobias, and St. James writes in his letter: *"Blessed is he that endureth temptation; for when he hath been tried, he shall receive the crown of life, which God hath promised to them that love him,"* and St. Peter says to us, *"Brethren, be sober and watch: because your adversary the devil, as a roaring lion goeth about seeking whom he may devour. Whom resist ye, strong in the faith..."*

Thus, do not be deceived by desolation (and all that it implies: dryness, discouragement, trouble, trials, temptations of all kinds). One must suffer in order to reach holiness.

The Schema of St. John of the Cross

At the beginning of his work The Ascent of Mt. Carmel, St. John of the Cross, in order to indicate the ascension of the soul towards the mystical ways, made a drawing illustrating this ascension.

1. At the bottom right, there is a long trail that ascends, descends, turns and comes to an impasse. In this way, St. John of the Cross wrote: *"human consolations."*

: I wanted to become a saint indeed, but I also would like my efforts to be recognized, my superiors to encourage me, etc... not to be left alone... and then it happens, and I leave all!

: Sir, you are on a dead-end street; you will never attain sanctity.

2. Another path turns left and right, climbs up and down and eventually ends up at the starting point. Underneath, the saint wrote: *"divine consolations."*

: No, I am not looking for human consolations, but when I meditate or go to Communion I would like to feel something sweet, some love for the good God, the joy of His presence, some sorrow for my sins, but I remain dry; I even have temptations and I feel like I am wasting my time: I'm going to drop my meditations!

St. Francis de Sales said to us: *"Do not seek the consolations of God; rather, seek the God of consolations."* You will never attain sanctity if you continue to confuse progress and spiritual consolation.

3. In the center (which takes up most of the page), he has what looks like a mine shaft. Narrow... black... upon which the saint had written five times in Spanish: "Nada, nada, nada, nada, nada (nothing)!" And it is the only road that leads to the top!

: But, Father, I have probably been deceived... I must at all costs do something else. I have terrible temptations... I am not making any progress! If you knew all the sentiments that are in my soul... I am losing the Faith... I feel like committing the most horrible sins, etc.

: Courage! You are on the right road!

: But it is impossible! My imagination is filled with thoughts of impurity and hatred. It seems to me that I do not believe in anything anymore.

: You are on the right track; do not leave it! Continue!

Then the top of the mine shaft opens out into a crater where there is light: St. John of the Cross wrote there: *"And there on top, still nothing!"* Another type of temptation, very different. One feels so far from the good God! One considers himself such a vile sinner! One would like to do better, but does not manage!

Finally at the very top, the green prairies of Mount Carmel watered by the seven gifts of the Holy Ghost, and producing the twelve fruits of the Holy Ghost!... Courage! Let nothing hinder you!

"Now what do we do?" St. Ignatius will show us:

<u>FIFTH RULE No. 318</u>

318: *In a period of distress we are not to alter anything, but should remain firm and unyielding in our resolutions and the purpose of mind in which we found ourselves on the day preceding such distress, or in the purpose in which we found ourselves in the preceding consolation. For, in times of comfort, it is the good angel that guides us by his counsel, whereas, in distress, it is the evil spirit; but the latter's counsel will never bring us to a right decision.*

How many catastrophes have taken place because this fifth rule has been ignored and forgotten!

It is Prohibited to Change Resolutions During the Time of Desolation

Why? Because it is then that the devil is active, and thus, if you follow the impulse of the devil, you are certain to do that which he desires. "Ordinarily," because we will see later on that there are false consolations which come from the devil. During true consolations it is always God who is acting. However, in this regard it is easy to make a mistake.

While in desolation, the desire to do evil is always a sign of the devil at work. (Remember the six odors or signs, of which we spoke in the second rule.)

How many vocations have been lost because this rule has been forgotten:

: Father, the poor little one does not feel like returning to the seminary. Is this not because he does not have a vocation?

: Beware! Does he have a vocation or not? That is another question. Now he is suffering an attack from the devil. It is not the time to leave. The devil is doing his work, and that can sometimes be a positive sign of a vocation. My friend, go back to the seminary. We will decide later if you have a vocation or not.

: And if I do not have a vocation?

: In a year or two, you will make a retreat and after being placed in the Ignatian indifference, that is, "God above all," you will then sort out the question of whether God is calling you or not. For the present, DO NOT CHANGE. I, poor Fr. Barrielle, when I was 17 years old, had the stupid idea of leaving the minor seminary. Luckily, my confessor told me to wait, otherwise I would not be here today.

How many people give up their resolutions at the first snare of the devil. What a pity! How can one avoid being fooled? Well, listen!

SIXTH RULE No. 319

THE GOLDEN RULE OF THE SPIRITUAL LIFE: THE COUNTERATTACK

319: *Though in principle we should not alter our previous resolutions in periods of distress, it is of great value to strive in a sense opposed to the distress; for instance by more insistence on prayer, meditation, close examination, and by making an effort to practice some appropriate penance.*

Not only is it necessary not to change one's resolutions during times of desolation, but one must not remain passive either. One must counterattack, otherwise the stream will carry one away. Let us re-examine the seminarian tempted to leave the seminary.

: Yes, I will be bored, I will be wasting my time, that will be unbearable, etc.

: No! No! You must not remain that way. See the false reasoning which is a sign of the devil: "Waste your time!" You will not waste your time, you will work hard. You will even obtain the salvation of many souls by your work and your prayers. Even if you do not have a priestly vocation and God is calling you to the lay state, you could very well work for the salvation of souls. All this is a sign of the devil. If the devil wants you to leave the seminary, it is not a sign that you do not have a vocation. You will not waste your time. You will continue your studies. You will be the best seminarian. Your will follow the rule as well as you can, you will communicate every day, you will reveal your conscience to your director, you will be generous, you will make sacrifices, and pray for sinners...

: And what if I do not have a vocation?

: Well then, in one or two years you will make a serious retreat to decide on your future, and there, God will enlighten you and give you the strength not to do **your will** but **the will of God.** As for now, behave as a seminarian and have a great devotion to the Blessed Virgin Mary. Work hard... That is what I call the "COUNTERATTACK."

The Blessed Fr. Peter Faber, a priest of Savoy, came to Paris to study for a doctorate in Theology at the Sorbonne. He was poor, so he rented a room with two other roommates: Xavier and Ignatius. He was a very pious priest. He soon realized that Ignatius, his elder and only a layman, was more advanced along the paths of sanctity. One day, when he had many temptations, (possibly of the flesh) Ignatius told him:

: I will teach you a secret on how to rid of the temptations. Meanwhile, the more temptations you will endure, the more you will advance in perfection.

: Teach me your secret!

: Well, as soon as you are tempted, multiply the acts of the opposite virtue. Are you tempted to gluttony? Fast! Tempted to anger? Keep quiet! To hate? Pray for your enemy! To pride? Humble yourself! To sensuality? Do penance!

That is how, in a short time, Fr. Faber became a saint. To the judgment of St. Ignatius, he was the best preacher of the retreat. It was he, Fr. Faber, that said the first Mass at Montmartre when the first Jesuits made their vows (he was the only priest, as Ignatius was not yet ordained).

St. Ignatius indicates four types of easy counterattack:

1. PRAYER.
2. MEDITATION.
3. FERVENT EXAMINATION OF CONSCIENCE. Often the devil makes us believe that we have sinned when, in fact, we have not only not consented but gained merit by resisting him. If there was a fault, the examination gives us confidence and makes us thank God and obtain pardon by an act of contrition and firm purpose of amendment.
4. A little PENANCE... some small penance will drive the devil away: for example, three Hail Marys while kneeling on your fingers, or a decade of the rosary with your arms

extended in the form of a cross, or a little sacrifice at table. The devil fears that. St. Benedict, one day, had a terrible temptation of the flesh and was unable to get rid of it. He took off his cowl and rolled in a patch of brambles. His body was covered with blood, but the devils had fled. This is an important principle necessary to conquer the devil.

How must one behave during temptation?

Are you tempted? Pray! At that moment, I warn you, it is not rare that the devil tries to pull "a fast one" and intensifies his temptation:

: "It is useless! I will get you once again... give in and I will leave you alone." Rather, intensify your prayers and let the devil have it. If he tempts you during the whole night, pray the whole night through. In the event of your succumbing to the temptation, at least you would have already decided to continue praying. If necessary, add some small penances, use holy water, invoke "Mary, terror of demons," St. Joseph, St. Michael, etc. Then at the moment when you felt that the fall was inevitable, all of a sudden, the temptation had left. What had happened? The devil, who does not like to be beaten, seeing that you were determined to pray, departed without notice.

Believe in Prayer! Ah! My friends, believe in prayer! We never can insist enough on this. A Christian never says: "There is nothing else to do." There remains always the great means of prayer, which is all powerful. It places the very Power of God in our own hands. One sees in the Gospels that Jesus took great care in teaching his own how to pray and, especially, **to give them faith in the efficacy of prayer.** *"Ask and you will receive, seek and you will find, knock and it will be opened to you."* It was also said in different ways: "To him who asks, it will be given, to him who knocks, it will be opened, he who seeks, will find," (Matt. 7; Mark 11; Luke 11; John 14+).

And which of you, if he ask his father bread, will he give him a stone? Or a fish, will he for a fish give him a serpent? Or if he shall ask an egg, will he reach him a scorpion? If you then, being evil, know how to give good gifts to your children, how much more will your Father from heaven give the good Spirit to them that ask Him? (Luke 11:11-13).

In this regard, Jesus tells us to press even further. We, for our part, would never dare be so insistent, had He not thus instructed us. Remember the parable of the irksome friend (Luke 11:5-8). In the middle of the night, a friend arrives, not having eaten. All the stores are closed, so he goes and knocks on his neighbor's door, saying "Lend me some bread."

: No, we are sleeping.
: You are not sleeping.
: Yes we are, leave us in peace.

And he continues to knock at the door. At last, the neighbor opens the window: "Here is your bread, let us sleep in peace!" Jesus said, "Do likewise with your Father in heaven." We would never have dreamed of doing such a thing, and He told us to do it. We find this lesson everywhere in the Gospel. Even after the Paschal meal, Jesus reproaches the disciples: *"Until now you have asked Me for nothing. Ask and you will receive. Whatever you ask the Father in my name, He will give it to you."*

Believe in the Efficacy of Prayer!

St. Alphonsus said: *"He who prays will be saved, he who does not pray will be damned!"* Words that must be engraved in the minds of children. Which of your children will you find in Heaven? Those who pray. How is it that, whereas God is infinite goodness, some Christians can still be damned? Alas! It is because they do not pray!

He who prays will be saved, he who does not pray will be damned, and St. Alphonsus adds this little jewel in his treatise on prayer: *"All the saints are in heaven because they have prayed much. They would be less holy if they had prayed less, and they would not have been there at all, if they had not prayed..."*

The saint adds these even more consoling words: *"All the damned are in hell because they have stopped praying!... They would not be there had they not stopped praying."*

If you happen to be at the bottom of the ocean and nobody even dreamed of you, pray! I do not know what the good God will do; what I do know is that He will come to your aid. I was one day at Chabeuil, and coming out of the chapel, one of the retreatants said to me, "Father, what you say is true. It happened to me!" He then explained to me how one day he was drowning in Lake Auvergne, and since he could not swim, his friends thought he had drowned. He had the idea of praying to the Blessed Virgin Mary. At that moment he felt something cold under his feet; it was a rock. He recovered his confidence and started thrashing about, thereby drawing the attention of his friends, who were on the point of leaving the place, having given up hope of finding him. They came back, and he was saved... What's more, the story is a true one!

While on this subject, allow me to share a very different experience with you. Once, I had one of the most painful experiences a priest can have on earth. I had been intimately involved with the apostasy of a fairly large number of confreres: seminarians, religious and, alas, some priests! Well, there is something that I can tell you: they had all (save few exceptions) ceased praying. Some of them, out of a zeal for souls, had left off praying... "Souls are waiting," etc.! Others, out of laziness, neglect, discouragement, or shame... They had all stopped praying. At that moment, the devil put a spanner in the works, and a catastrophe happened. *"Nemo Repente Fit Pessimus,"* said St. Bernard. "Nobody becomes evil all of a sudden." One of the first things the devil always does is to make people stop praying. No more meditations, spiritual reading, rosaries, examinations of conscience, breviary, thanksgivings, visits to the Blessed Sacrament, confessions... No more Masses (or sacrilegious ones, which is worse!). No more devotion to the Blessed Virgin Mary, etc. At that time, they were ripe for a catastrophe!

St. Alphonsus recommends that, because God always listens to all our prayers, we must ask daily for the grace to always pray every day! That is why, amongst other things, devotion to Mary will have saved so many sinners. God listens to the littlest prayer. *"Si quis tristetur, oret,"* said St. James (5:3): "If any one is sad, he must pray." *"Hoc genus demoniorum non ejicitur nisi jejunio et oratione,"* said Jesus, talking about the young lunatic; "This type of devil, (especially the one of impurity) is driven out only by fasting and prayer." Jesus says often: *Vigilate Et Orate:* "Watch and pray."

SEVENTH RULE No. 320

320: *When in distress, a man should reflect that God is testing him by leaving him to his own resources in his struggle against the different assaults and temptations of the enemy; he can succeed with the help of God, which is always there, even though he is not clearly aware of it. God has indeed withdrawn any great warmth of feeling, intensity of love and extraordinary grace, but He has left grace enough for the man's eternal salvation.*

Do not believe that all is lost because Our Lord is hiding, like the spouse in the Canticle of Canticles: *Who "hides behind a lattice and takes pleasure in making his spouse search for him."* For sure, Our Lord will never leave you without sufficient grace. (Attention, we are talking about **sufficient grace.**)

THE TEMPTATION OF ST. CATHERINE OF SIENA

This great privileged and mystical virgin, who had continual visions and profound mystical graces, by the permission of God, became prey to a most horrible temptation. God allowed the devil to assail her. She suffered the most wicked thoughts and even sensations (as the devil can, God permitting, excite our instincts). Catherine prayed, and begged God not to abandon her. She protested that she would rather die than commit a sin. The devil said to her: "It is useless; you will not be able to resist... besides, you have already sinned, and God has abandoned you, etc."

: Oh! Lord, help me! I would rather die or suffer than offend You in any way!

It was diabolical, but all of a sudden the temptation stopped! (Never forget that a temptation does not last one moment longer than God wants it to last.) Then Our Lord appeared to her; as usual, He spoke to her familiarly, and she gently reproached Him:

: Oh, my good Master, You abandoned me during the most dreadful moment of my life!

: Catherine, I did not abandon you!

: Where were You, Lord?

: I was in your heart.

: In my heart? With all the filth in it?
: Did you consent to it?
: Oh! No, my Lord! You know that I would suffer anything rather than offend You... even die...
: Well then, know that it was I who supported you and took pleasure in seeing your fidelity in front of the devil. Do you think that I would have abandoned you?

In our temptations, we must never forget this example taken from the life of this great saint.

EIGHTH RULE No. 321

321: *In this state he should also strive to abide in patience, which is the antidote to the trials that beset him. He should also reflect that he will soon be comforted, and should put forth all his efforts against this distress, as described in the sixth rule.*

When we are tempted, *"have patience!"* Patience means: to suffer and wait... but also, to have *confidence* and *hope!*

Never forget that our holy religion is the religion of the "Our Father." Do not forget the two wings that little St. Theresa speaks of. We need both of them: *self-diffidence and confidence in God.* With these wings we will climb high without danger. See what Jesus said in the Sermon on the Mount to those who fear that they will have not the necessary food and clothing (Mt. 6).

St. Ignatius even promises tempted souls who trust in God that the temptation will soon be followed with sweet consolations, provided that the soul applies itself to the observance of the sixth rule, with the hope of soon being consoled. The sixth rule is that of the counterattack; do not forget it.

St. Paul, in First Corinthians 10, tells us something that should keep us from all discouragement: *"God is faithful, who will not suffer you to be tempted above that which you are able: but will make also with temptation issue, that you may be able to bear it."* This is why, in the case of martyrdom, Jesus forbids us to think ahead of time. On that day, if He calls us to that honor, we will have the necessary graces. *"The Holy Ghost will answer for you."*

NINTH RULE No. 322

Why Does the Good God Permit Temptation?

When we are tempted we must ask ourselves why. Only then will we make progress. Sometimes it is because of our faults, sometimes for natural reasons we could, and should, have evaded. Other times, it is just God's initiative wanting us to merit by these graces. Hence the need of an examination of conscience. Those who do not keep this practice deprive themselves of many graces for their sanctification. Here is the ninth rule of St. Ignatius:

322: *There are three principle reasons why we experience distress:*

a) Because we are listless, apathetic and careless in our spiritual exercises; it is on account of our own faults that our spiritual consolation is withdrawn.

b) To test our worth, and to show how far we are able to advance in God's service and praise without that great reward of comforts and extraordinary favors.

c) To give us clear understanding and insight, to enable us to have a deep inner conviction that, of ourselves, we are powerless to produce or sustain a flood of devout feelings, intense love, tears or any spiritual consolation, but that this is all a gratuitous gift of God our Lord. We are not, that is, to build on another's foundations, getting above ourselves in pride and empty boasting, claiming as our own the devout feelings or other features of spiritual consolations.

There are three principle causes: which means that there could be others. For example there could be natural causes.

Many people get angry easily simply because they have not slept enough;

it is not uncommon. A superior was once appointed as head of a small hospital in a busy area. They had had there some sisters who were frequently angry, in a bad mood or argumentative. Now, this is not the way that sisters should behave. The superior, watching the conduct of these very devoted and generous souls, wondered why they acted thus. She finally understood that these sisters were just lacking sleep. There was a shortage of personnel, and these sisters took from their sleep to make up for the shortage. The result was that, afterwards, they exploded like a champagne cork for mere trifles. The superior ordered that they were to sleep an extra half hour and that nobody was to keep any night vigils without permission. From that day on, as if by an extraordinary effect, the sisters did not argue any more!

St. Theresa of Avila, when a sister came to her saying, "Mother, I have had a vision," said, "Good, tomorrow you will have beef bouillon for supper." (Something that in the reformed Carmel was never done.) Another time, a steak was advised for a sister who thought she had had a vision. For someone leading a sedentary life, the lack of exercise can be the cause of scruples and troubles.

Fr. Timon David, founder of the First Patronage for Workers, in a work written after the French Revolution, in his admirable treatise "On the Confession and Direction of Young People," tells us that one must pay close attention to those with tuberculosis. Why this? Because of their inactivity and malnutrition, they are prone to terrible temptations which hinder their cure and lead them to hell. Give them good books, teach them to contemplate the mysteries of the Rosary, tell them to practice the presence of God, to flee from dangerous dreams, to communicate and confess frequently. Their sickness will then help them to fulfill God's plan in becoming saints. All these natural causes boil down to three principle causes:

1. Punishment.

You will realize, after spending a few hours in front of a television set or by omitting your spiritual reading, that the following day your meditation is dry. Take note... do not repeat it, or else Jesus will keep quiet; this alone is a great punishment. If you have had violent temptations after having gone near the beach, or after having read a certain magazine, or after watching a film, or daydreaming, or uselessly prolonging your siesta, or after having taken too much food, or drunk too much coffee (or cocktails), reflect and take note... This is how one manages to live a serious interior life. When you pray faithfully the rosary, you may feel or understand in what way your family is sinning. Inform everyone immediately.

2. Desolation or temptation could very well be an occasion to Practice Heroic Virtue, rather than a punishment.

Take for example, the temptation of St. Joseph, the tribulations of the Holy Family. They were not punishments. Yet, they suffered vehemently! If the Holy Family had not suffered these temptations, we would have been deprived of heroic examples.

St. Theresa of the Child Jesus, on her death bed, had terrible temptations against the Faith. "I am in a tunnel...," she told her sister, Mother Agnes. She endeavored to repeat with an invincible faith (while feeling nothing), "My God, I love you! My God, I love you!" For sure, it was not a punishment; she had not read the writings of Sartre, Gide, de Beavoir, Sagan or any of that rubbish. The good Lord wanted her to gain merit in order to drop a more abundant rain of roses for the conversion of unbelievers. That is why He allowed all the demons to kick out against her.

You, yourself, may also have to suffer certain trials in order to save a son, a friend, etc. Accept them humbly and generously. The Curé of Ars, on the eve of the conversion of some big sinner, used to suffer furious attacks from the devil.

3. A Lesson.

These trials may be given to teach us a lesson. We are all more or less prone to keep to ourselves the credit of a good. This God finds unbearable. We steal what belongs to Him. *"My glory, I will give to no one else,"* He tells us by the mouth of the prophet Isaiah, (Is:42) and St. Paul writes (I Cor:4): *"Or what hast thou and that thou hast not received? And if thou hast received, why dost thou glory as if thou hadst not received it?"*

: I am the best parishioner!...

: Well, you would not have had such a grace, if you did not have such a mother, or that priest. What, then, would have become of you?

How good the good God is for preventing us from falling into such an error! He allows us to be tempted to commit sins capable of sending us to the bottom of hell. After that, we will not be tempted to despise anyone.

Humble yourself and thank the good God, but *"vigilate et orate."* Everything must help toward one's sanctification.

TENTH AND ELEVENTH RULE
Nos. 323 and 324

: And when all is going well, what shall we do?
: Well! Take advantage of it to practice the virtues and gain merits. On a bicycle, with a tail wind, one profits to gain miles, so that, when the wind turns, the distance will have already been covered.

323: *In a period of consolation a man should think about his conduct in the distress that will ensue, building up his strength afresh for that experience.*

Above all humble yourself! Not just a little, as much as you possibly can.

324: *When experiencing consolation he should be careful to keep himself humble and modest, recalling how worthless he is in times of distress, when he is without the favor of this comfort. Contrariwise, a man who is in a state of distress should reflect that he can do a great deal with the grace that is sufficient to withstand all his enemies, finding strength in his Creator and Lord.*

"I can do all in Him who strengthens me," said St. Paul.

The Venerable Marine d'Escobar, a well known Spanish mystic, was one day following the Spiritual Exercises of St. Ignatius, when the Archangel Gabriel appeared to her and congratulated her on making the exercises which Our Lady herself had given to St. Ignatius. The Archangel added: "Mary herself lived these rules during her life." Someone who does not know the life of the Blessed Virgin, who has not meditated on it, or who does not understand the Exercises may think that it is an exaggeration. But if one contemplates carefully, it is clear that she did behave in this way. Take the Visitation. Her old cousin said to her, "And whence is this that the Mother of my Lord should come to me?" What was Mary's reaction? She directed the glory to God: "My soul doth magnify the Lord... the Almighty hath done great things in me...," and she humbled herself as much as she could: "He hast regarded the humility of His handmaid" (literally, "His slave").

Let us make sure to remain humble when all is going well. The more we receive great graces, the more we should ask for humiliations, especially the third degree of humility... if we do not, our treasure is in jeopardy. That is why one must not be self-complacent, one must not make known to others the precious graces we have received; otherwise, what happened to Ezechias will also happen to us. He showed his treasures to the ambassador of the Assyrian king, and Isaias reproved his self-complacency, saying to him: "You unfortunate! He himself will come to take away all your treasure."

TWELFTH RULE No. 325

It is a very important rule which completes the sixth (No. 319).

325: *The enemy is like a woman, weak in face of opposition, but correspondingly strong when not opposed. In a quarrel with a man, it is natural for a woman to lose heart and run away when he faces up to her; on the other hand, if the man begins to be afraid and to give ground, her rage, vindictiveness and fury overflow and know no limit. In the same way, it is typical of the enemy to collapse and lose heart, his assaults turning tail, when a man who is training himself in the spiritual ways faces up to the enemy's assaults, doing the precise opposite of what is suggested. On the other hand, if the retreatant begins to feel panic and to lose heart at these assaults, there is no animal on earth so savage as is the enemy of our human nature in the ever-growing malice with which he carries out his evil plan.*

The devil becomes terrible if he sees us hesitate. For example, a seminarian who hesitates concerning his vocation: "And if I interrupt my seminary for a couple of months? I will be more experienced in the ways of the world and that will make me stronger." The devil will suggest to him good reasons; if he hesitates, he is lost. The devil then sets up greater temptations: a good opportunity...an occasion for marriage...health troubles, etc.

Remember the principle of Fr. Terradas: "One must not play with the devil." In the same vein, if your wife starts to look at her clothes and desires to shorten them by just such a little bit, soon she will be immodest just like all the others. Or, if husband and wife after some fights, begin to wonder whether this could be sufficient grounds for divorce, the devil will get the ball rolling by any means so as to lead to a catastrophe. If he feels that they want to do "like everyone else," the demons will be let loose. As hard as they may try not to sin, the devil will get his way and lead them into a sinful life.

St. Augustine has a famous saying which sums up the devil's play: *"Latrare potest, mordere non potest nisi volentem."* "He is able to bark, but not to bite unless allowed to." If you live in a rural area, as I did, you may have some experience with dogs. You find a dog charging you, barking furiously. What should you do? If you run away, the dog will certainly bite you. What must you do? Face him calmly without showing that you are afraid. The dog, vexed at seeing you calm, will lower his head, diminish his barking and turn tail. If, however, you had shown any fear, in as much as he feels you hesitate, he will become more ferocious and bite you. Never forget the principle:

IN THE PRESENCE OF A TEMPTATION, DO NOT BE DISTURBED,
NEVER CHANGE YOUR RESOLUTIONS.

Do not give in, even a little bit, as St. Ignatius said, "do whatever is diametrically opposed to what the devil suggests." Pray, multiply acts of the contrary virtue, etc.

St. Vincent de Paul became a saint because of the Exercises of St. Ignatius which he followed in 1611, a fact generally ignored by the public at large. From then on they were propagated in all his houses. He himself followed the fifteen day Exercises twice a year and was saved from a temptation because of this rule. There was in Paris a young teacher of philosophy who was about to lose the Faith. Fr. Vincent asked God to deliver the teacher from his temptations and to give them rather to himself. The request was granted, and, despite the fact that he was a priest and a saint, he had the most terrible temptations against the Faith that one can have. At all times, while saying his Mass, preaching, during meditation, while working with the poor, all the tricks that the devil could invent against the Faith assailed him continually. "You are not loyal, there is no God, Our Lord is not in the Host, you are telling lies." What did he do? Should he have opened his theology manuals to check whether he had studied all the proofs? He would have gone mad, for the devil is wicked! This is what the saint did: he applied the twelfth rule. He wrote an act of faith, with very ardent words, asking God that he die a martyr for the Holy Faith. He signed the paper and pinned it over his heart and promised that each time he placed his hand over his heart, it would mean that he repeated his offering to die a martyr for the Faith. Whenever he was tempted, he would place his hand over his heart and, thus, thousands of times, he would make an act of faith, both sublime and heroic. The devil, seeing that all his temptations, far from succeeding in making him sin, rather made him perform heroic acts, finally left him in peace. Do not forget this rule; it is a capital one during temptations.

THIRTEENTH RULE No. 326

The devil imitates a seducer: "Do not tell your father, do not tell your husband. Otherwise, your game will be up from the very beginning." In the same way, the devil fears that his traps will be revealed to our confessor, or spiritual director, or to a man of God who is familiar with his tricks.

326: *He is also like a seducer in his desire to remain disguised and undetected. If that sort of schemer pays dishonorable court to the daughter of a good father or the wife of a good husband, he wants his words and suggestions not to be disclosed; he is greatly upset if the daughter or the wife tells the father or the husband about his deceitful words and his dishonorable purpose, since he easily recognizes that he will not then realize the plan he has embarked on.*

So is it with the enemy of our human nature. When he introduces into a faithful soul his lying suggestions, he is very anxious that these should be accepted and kept secret. But he is far from pleased when their victim discloses them to a good confessor or someone else versed in spiritual matters, who is acquainted with the ill-disposed designs of the tempter, who then realizes that his wicked attempt must fail, once his obvious tricks are revealed.

"If this soul reveals everything to an enlightened confessor..." Remark the attributive "enlightened," because, today especially, one can come across a confessor who understands nothing about the direction of souls. Others abuse their role, as St. Paul already warned Timothy (I Tim. 4; II Tim. 3).

St. Theresa of Avila had much to suffer from un-enlightened confessors and wrote in her autobiography in Chapter 13: "It is important that the master be judicious, that he have right judgment, and that he be experienced and, if this is joined with sanctity, the mixture is perfect... a soul should rather stay without a director until she find one such as described."

St. Jeanne de Chantal was very confused by a good Capuchin confessor who had her take an eccentric and forbidden vow. He terrorized her. Luckily, she met St. Francis de Sales. The bishop of Geneva was well known. He was sent by the Duke of Savoy as an ambassador to Henry IV of France, and, as he passed through Dijon, the bishop was invited to stop at the home of the president of the parliament, Mr. Fremiot. At another time, the saint was invited to preach for Lent. Lady Fremiot, a widow of Chantal and daughter of the president, was spending Lent at her father's house in order to follow the sermons of the holy preacher. "Your excellency, I have a confessor who does not want me to consult anyone else... I may be committing a mortal sin if I talk to you."

: Go ahead, talk! Do not be afraid...

: But he made me take a vow never to go to another confessor; he demands that I do nothing without telling him, without asking his permission. He told me that if I did consult someone else I would commit a mortal sin. Perhaps I was wrong to tell you, perhaps I will be damned?

: No, no. Do not worry, go ahead, talk.

In the end, smiling at her, St. Francis said, "Get rid of your confessor. He understands nothing." Thank goodness, otherwise we would have had one more crazy person; instead, we got one more saint.

Another example. One day at Chabeuil, a young man came to me on the first night of his retreat: "Father, I believe that I must leave. I come in disobedience. My confessor forbade me to come here, as he does not agree with Chabeuil."

I asked him whether he had any nervous disorder.

: No, Father!

: Well then, your confessor does not have the right to forbid you to come to a retreat house which is approved by the local ordinary and where the Exercises preached have been approved by all the popes from Paul III to Pius XII (this was during his reign). It is an abuse of authority. You do not have to do what your confessor says.

The young man made a very good retreat. One must know that one always has the right to change doctors and, likewise, to go without permission to another confessor.

St. Theresa of Avila was very confused by confessors who understood nothing of her case relevant to mystical theology. She was reassured by the learned Dominicans and Jesuits who were not her confessors but knew her mystical theology. They reassured her that her visions, ecstasies and prayers were from God.

This having been said, do not make me say what I never meant to say. Do not hide anything from your confessor or your spiritual director; the more the devil finds reasons for you not to tell him something, the more you must tell him.

I know cases in which the devil managed to make people lose their vocation because they kept quiet concerning some childish detail, apparently of no importance. If the young man had revealed this detail, the devil's plan would have been thwarted. Even if, and especially if, the devil prevents you from revealing an insignificant detail, go and tell your director. Tell him that you had to stand on bricks to jump over the wall, that you have her photograph in your wallet, that you telephone her each evening, that you have some of her hair, etc.

: But I will not do it again! I will put the bricks away... I do not want to disturb my confessor, he is very busy, he will probably laugh at me, etc.

: No, go and tell all!

Or, you could consult a specialist, or an old priest, or a missionary whom you have known for a long time: an old parish priest who knows your problem or knows the family, or a retreat-master who counseled you frequently. Moreover, you will find those who prefer not to speak to a priest and who will come to you with their troubles. They know you and they have confidence in you; they are just not used to talking to a cleric. Do not hesitate to place yourself at their disposal and help them out; and if need be, tell them: "Do not worry, I am going to take you to a priest who will sort it out easily." One sometimes forgets that the first director of a conscience of a wife is her husband. St. Paul said: "Women must keep quiet in church, and at home, she must consult her husband." Those women who are self-opinionated and uncompromising with their husbands deprive themselves of many graces, even if they do go to Communion every day and spend an hour in the confessional every week. How many spouses, on the other hand, mutually help one another by praying together and asking each other about their scruples, worries and things on their mind. As to the Spiritual Exercises, it is better that they follow them separately, alone with God. The necessary exchange between spouses should not be done during a retreat, this would be a mistake. If not, the retreat risks being broken and becoming a second honeymoon... When at home, they should help one another. How many wives and husbands have been the cause of one another's conversion!

Keep the habit of revealing your temptations to your confessor. Do not wait until you have succumbed to them before you tell him. Often, the fact of having laid bare one's temptation chases away the tempter and his traps.

FOURTEENTH RULE No. 327

327: *Or, again, he acts like a military commander in his attempts to overcome and seize the object he has set his heart on. An officer in command of any army takes up a position, makes a reconnaissance to discover the strength and disposition of troops in a fortified post, and launches his attack at the weakest point. Similarly, the enemy of our human nature makes a tour of inspection of our virtues - theological, cardinal and moral. Where he finds us the weakest and most defective in what pertains to our eternal salvation, he attacks at that point, seeking to overthrow us.*

A commander-in-chief who wants to attack a town sends in his spies first, to find the weakest and least fortified point before he decides where to attack. Likewise, the devil "roams about us," as St. Peter says, looking for our weak points in order to attack them. Thus, we can know ahead of time where he will strike.

You like to eat... to drink... to be lazy... or you are imprudent, you read anything indiscriminately... you do not select your friends carefully, etc. How many catastrophes have started by slight imprudence!

I have known people filled with great qualities and virtues. They only had a very small fault. They were a little too sensitive to criticism. One day their parish priest reproached them, with or without reason. They left all, even the practice of religion! This was surely the work of the devil. When you observe so many priests, religious and Christians, well-advanced in the interior life, who later stagnate or even slide backwards, you wonder why. Whence did it come about? Out of a major difficulty? No! There was a slight inordinate attachment: gluttony or, more frequently, human respect, this accursed human respect which is the source of laxity and even of the damnation of so many people, even amongst the clergy... the fear of being smiled at by a confrere!

We will have lost our health for an insignificant thing, whereas we could have had the courage to make great sacrifices! A doctor of a convent in Barcelona said one day to Fr. Vallet: "I do not understand. Here are women who have left fortunes, castles, etc., and yet they become attached to a small picture or get angry about a reproach. What is more, this hinders them in their sanctification!"

Fr. Vallet said to us: *"I BEG YOU TO LOOK AND SEE WHAT YOUR HABITUAL VENIAL SINS ARE! IT IS BY THESE THAT THE DEVIL KEEPS A GRIP ON YOU."*

It is a rule always to be used, especially on retreat and when about to take one's resolutions.

* * * * *

Rules of Discernment for the
SECOND WEEK

(Other rules which deal in more depth with the matter of discernment of spirits.) These rules are more fitting for the second week.

The rules of the first week are elementary rules for everyone: sinners, beginners and advanced souls. Ordinarily, with souls advanced in the interior life, the devil uses more subtle tactics. Thus, it becomes more difficult to discover the plans of the devil because, in general, he tempts souls under the appearance of good. He does not suggest to them evil deeds; rather, he suggests good ones to them. How could anyone resist such an invitation? Do we have the right to refuse to do good? Would this not be a fault of pusillanimity or of laziness? And yet, how many zealous apostles, how many good works, have been thrown away for good reasons, skillfully suggested by the seducer, disguised as "an angel of light?"

These rules will be useful to all generous souls, even if still in the ascetical ways. (Asceticism means a combat. These souls are in the ascetical ways who live in the ordinary ways of Christian virtue with the aid of the Holy Ghost, which is always necessary for supernatural action.)

These rules will be even more useful to those whom God has already raised to the mystical ways, where they are led, completely given up to Him by the gifts of the Holy Ghost, rather than by ordinary combats. These rules are also applicable to special cases of miracles, visions, mystical states, and ecstasies, which are not necessarily signs of sanctity. "Otherwise," said St. Bonaventure with some humor, "one would have to say that Balam was a saint and his ass as well!" Ecstasies are divine signs which are performed rather for the good of the people than for that of the soul in ecstasy himself.

One must not desire these miraculous states, as they are often accompanied by terrible trials. If the soul is not detached from all, these graces could be harmful. Fr. Vallet said: "We are all called to the ordinary mystical union where the Holy Ghost leads us by His gifts, but not all of us are called to the miraculous mystical union. When God calls someone to such a state, he must accept it **humbly** and with great **fidelity**."

No matter which way we are dealing with, ascetical or mystical, ordinary or extraordinary union, these rules, which demand a close study, may help souls very much, either in reassuring them, or in thwarting the devil's traps. They indeed give us at least some of the signs which reveal the presence of the good angel, as well as that of the evil spirit. It goes without saying that if these rules are not accompanied by prayer and docility to the Holy Ghost, we will often fall into one of the devil's traps. (Hence, another reason for meditating on the rules of the second week.) All too often, people talk about the graces *"gratis datae"* (ecstasies, miracles, visions, gift of tongues, etc.) in different ways. The clergy and the learned tend to deny or scorn them, often out of the fear of appearing too credulous. Others run after apparitions and imagine that the Blessed Virgin Mary will bring something new into the Church which it did not receive from her divine Son, as if Revelation did not end with the death of the last Apostle.

The learned Gerson, we saw, despised the visions of St. Catherine of Siena and wanted the Council of Constance to condemn all her revelations and visions and to order that no one speak any more about them. At the time of St. Theresa of Avila, all the learned people gathered together to discuss her visions and unanimously concluded that these favors were not from God. They even sent a delegation to notify her that she had been deceived by the devil, and that she take every means to leave this path, which they asserted was just an illusion.

One of the greatest difficulties encountered by the efforts to spread the Sacred Heart devotion was the fact that Our Lord made use of a humble Visitation sister to ask for the institution of this feast, the first Fridays of the month, the consecration, etc.

Yet in both the Old and the New Testaments, ineffable relations of God with certain men are often recounted. It is true that one must be careful about being too credulous. St. Peter, in his second epistle, after having recalled the vision of the Transfiguration on Mount Thabor, gives a grand rule which should be the guideline for all apparitions or extraordinary events: *"Sed habemus firmiorem propheticum sermonem."* In other words, we have, above all private revelation, the hierarchical and official Church, with the Deposit of the Faith. This should be the yardstick used in examining whether a vision is from God or not. Beware, as soon as the passions become mixed-up, many want to make you believe that the authentic hierarchy has spoken, while it is perhaps only a member of the hierarchy who may have, in fact, exceeded his powers.

The pope, speaking *ex cathedra,* is infallible. A bishop, even while having the role of the hierarchy in his diocese, is not necessarily infallible.

A bishop can make territorial laws, and must obey them when in his territory (at least, his subjects must). When it comes to strangers, canon law specifies that in certain cases, strangers passing-through are held in conscience to obey these laws, and in other cases they are not. A bishop is not able to pronounce *ex cathedra* (if there is nothing objectionable in matters of faith and morals) upon the truth of a particular divine favor, a vision, etc. The Holy Office, which twice condemned Padre Pio, has now allowed the introduction of his process of beatification.

In other words, *true obedience* and *the rule of faith* are the two rules used to judge whether a vision is true or not. With respect to personal miraculous graces, it will often be impossible to obtain a certitude, and the Church, while favoring public acts of devotion, pilgrimages, etc., avoids definitive pronouncements in such events.

We may give general rules in regard to mysticism: God is master! He acts as He pleases. The rules of discernment of St. Ignatius help us to act prudently in all cases (ascetical, ordinary mystical, and extraordinary mystical).

FIRST RULE No. 329

329: *The characteristic effect produced by God and His angels in their spiritual operations is a genuine lightness of heart and spiritual joy, eliminating all the disturbing sadness engendered by the enemy, whilst his characteristic activity is to resist such lightness of heart and spiritual consolation, alleging specious reasons, subtle suggestions and sophistries without end.*

St. Paul (Gal. 5:22) indicates the fruits of the Holy Ghost (twelve in the Vulgate and nine in the Greek texts), the first ones being charity, peace of soul and joy.

God and His angels give to the soul peace and joy (but St. Ignatius specifies a TRUE happiness). True spiritual joy is well-distinguished from a troubled joy, both dissipated and dissipating, which says, for example: "The Christian religion is one of joy; therefore, let us enjoy promiscuous dancing, a dissipated life, co-education, etc." Beware! It is not the true joy.

As soon as the devil arrives on the scene, he endeavors to rob the soul of its peace and joy (he does not always succeed with souls wholly given over to God). He tries to trouble the soul and make it sad... simply because he himself is eternally sad. This feeling one has of being invaded by sadness is, thus, a way of discerning the devil's presence. How does he do this? It is worth noticing.

"By specious reasons." These are not true, but only apparent, reasons. Many allow themselves to be taken in by them, but they prove nothing. It is false reasonings that have been the cause of the present troubles in the Church and which are throwing society into the greatest confusion ever known in history. The false reasons trouble much those with good dispositions, to the point of paralyzing their reaction on the grounds of their being faithful to their duties of state. A good example of this is the heretical catechism, which some have succeeded in imposing on the Church, despite the fact that it has been condemned on many occasions. Under the alleged pretext of a new and better method of teaching (which is truly good in itself), or under the pretext of a commission or a sub-commission which is not controlled, they have had this catechism published. Then they make the bishops believe that since they are part of collegiality, they have to accept that which was published by the sub-commission. Then they make the people believe that they are bound in conscience to accept, under pain of disobedience, that which their bishop has just published.

They suggest (some even dare to say it outright) that the Council has changed the Faith. This is a doctrine distinctly Modernist. They even go so far as to menace the booksellers, by withdrawing their patronage if they dare to sell the old catechisms. This amounts to a "Nazi" type of ecclesiastical officiousness, besides being contrary to justice and a grave abuse of authority.

Thus the trick was done; let us now analyze it.

Even if a bishop, God forbid, obliged a Christian, above the age of reason, to ignore the truths absolutely necessary for salvation, his orders would be null and void. However, not only did the bishops never give such orders, they even admitted that this new catechism was published against their wishes.

The sub-commissions, which try to impose the new catechism on us, give the following reasons, which would be valid if:

1. The bishops were imposing it (which is not the case).
2. These bishops gave commands with full authority. However, they never had the intention of giving commands which favored heresy.
3. What was commanded was not sinful.

This is what we call mystification! i.e. the fabrication of man-made mysteries:

: You do not receive Communion in the hand? You dare to disapprove of it? Well, then, you are defying your bishop...

: But, my bishop said he was opposed to Communion in the hand. The Holy Father stated that the greater number of bishops were against it. The authorization was given only for those areas where the custom was already established, whereas, here, it is not a custom. It is true that the innovators went on the attack: my bishop was warned that he could not go against the college of bishops. Then he published this authorization. Immediately, they made the religious and the children obey "the Council." They then threatened those parish priests who "disobeyed" their bishop and the Council. Was all this really from God? I myself do not believe so.

There is an example of a country parish priest, zealous, but confused by another man-made mystery of Catholic Action. I went to preach a recollection there and the priest, as soon as I had entered, asked my advice about a point that was worrying him. He had received an order from the 'Federation of Catholic Youth' ordering its adherents to go to the dances. He obeyed, thinking that even if it did not please him, he should obey. His problem now was that, since the youths had acquired a taste for dancing, one had joined the Communist cell in town, while many others had stopped going to Communion on Sundays.

Firstly, I said to him: "Father, you have not obeyed. Who should command around here? Above all, it is the bishop." Now, each year the bishop had officially forbidden youth dances, and that particular year he had done so twice.

Secondly, FALSE REASONS: "Father, instead of gathering youth at a dance, could you not see them after Mass or at a cafe? Or at their homes or in the fields? Do you really believe that the most favorable moment to approach them is when they have a young lady in their arms?"

Thirdly, look what happened! One has become a Communist, others do not communicate anymore. They do not even have the desire to communicate now that they have a taste for dancing. What apparent reasons! What subtleties! What continual illusions! It is the case of the fisherman who allows himself to be caught by the fish!

SECOND RULE No. 330

330: *Spiritual consolation with no previous occasion giving rise to it comes from our Lord God alone. It is the Creator's prerogative to come into and leave the soul, to move it with inspirations of love for His Divine Majesty. "With no previous occasion" means without any preceding awareness or knowledge of anything which might induce such consolation in the soul, by means of its own acts of intellect and will.*

Only God can perform miracles... true miracles, without a previous cause. God alone can create, that is, make something out of nothing. God alone can give and take away life. A creature can never create, make something out of nothing, even if it be only a sun ray. One must be aware that the devils are able to do certain secondary 'miracles' which are not truly miracles. They are only miracles relative to us, in that the devils are very much more intelligent and powerful than we are. God alone can perform a true miracle.

For example, God alone can raise a dead person to life, that is, one truly dead. Now if a fakir is not really dead, the devil is able to keep him in the state of apparent death even for a whole year and then, suddenly, "raise" him to life. If the fakir is truly dead, the devil would not be able to "raise" him to life. In the same way, great miracles done at a distance without the use of any instrument are proper to God as, for example, to restore sight without a physically functional eye, or to bring back to life an infant that was cut into pieces, as did St. Vincent Ferrer. God alone can do these. Take the case of Simon the Magician, who levitated as much as a thousand feet above the ground without any apparent assistance. Man, of his own strength, is unable to perform such acts, but the devils, who are not subject to the laws of gravity, can easily lift a person, as they clearly did with Simon. This instance happened during the life of St. Peter the Apostle and is recounted by Pope St. Clement. Simon the Magician, in order to counter St. Peter, had announced the day and the hour that he would raise himself to Heaven from a certain public place. St. Peter sent a young cleric, who was to succeed him as pope (St. Linus) to be a witness. The place was filled with people. Simon arrived and, behold, he ascended one thousand feet into the air. Miracle! (We will see, however, that the devil is able to perform miracles only with the permission of God.) For, while Simon was raised up there, God ordered the devil to let him go, so that he was smashed into the ground, to the great astonishment of the crowd.

One can recognize the prodigies (**not** the miracles) of the devil by four signs. They are important to remember, in order not to be taken-in by pseudo-miracles.

1. The devil and the demons cannot perform real miracles; they can only perform miracles relative to us, in the sense that they are stronger than we.
2. Their miracles are not for a good purpose: for example, the sorcerer who casts spells on cow's milk.
3. Generally, these pseudo-miracles favor bad doctrine: for example, Appolonius of Tiane, who made statues dance.
4. The devils are only able to perform them with the permission of God, and only as long as God allows it. God ordered the devil to let go of Simon the Magician, and he fell in front of the crowd, which was surprised to see him ascend and even more surprised to see him fall.

Why does the good God permit these pseudo-miracles of the devil? In order to punish those who refuse the true miracles and follow the sorcerer's incantations instead. *"Perdam sapientiam sapientium et prudentiam prudentium reprabo."* Or, as St. Paul says, "I will confound the wisdom of the wise and the prudence of the prudent. I will condemn it" (I Cor. 1:14).

The devils are able to produce false stigmata, to cause sweats of blood, and to carry a host from the hand of a priest to the tongue of a 'seer.' All this, the devil can do, as can the good angels. As St. John says: *"Test the spirits and keep only that which is good"* (1 John 4:1). In the same way, the devils are able to act upon the sensitive faculties, but they cannot enter our soul and compel our assent. How good is God to safeguard the citadel of our soul! The devil has no way of knowing what we think, unless we reveal it to him. He cannot compel our assent: we remain free.

God sometimes allows him to possess someone, to command his body and direct his person; yet, the devil cannot oblige the possessed soul to consent. That is way obsession, in which the devil solicits evil from the outside, sometimes in a prodigious way, is more frightening than possession. For, the possessed soul is a witness of the devil's action upon its own faculties and cannot be held responsible for it.

"Without a Preceding Cause."

For example, Blessed Anna-Maria Taigi, while in the kitchen, all of a sudden received lights on the Blessed Trinity. She went to see her confessor and told him about the illuminations she had had. Her confessor asked: "Have you read recently a book on the Blessed Trinity? Have you heard a conference? Did you pass in front of a church?..."

: No, it happened all of a sudden.

: If there are no preceding causes, then it is from God!

THIRD RULE No. 331

331: *Granted some occasion, a sense of consolation may be produced in the soul either by the good angel or the bad one, though with opposing ends in view. The good angel has in view the soul's progress, that it may grow by advancing from what is good to what is better. The evil spirit, contrariwise, tries to draw it to his own perverted designs and wickedness of will.*

In the beginning, one does not perceive what is going on. The tree is recognized by its fruits. Do not forget the principle that the devil wants to push us to evil, even if in the beginning he moves to do good. That is why the French saying declares, "The best is sometimes the enemy of the good."

The good angel, on the contrary, wants only the good. We must, therefore, study closely and attentively.

FOURTH RULE No. 332

It is a characteristic tactic of the devil when he wishes to fool a fervent soul: he does not suggest to him evil deeds. He suggests to him to do good, but not any type of good deed, only that good deed which suits his taste. One likes to do that which he does well, and then little by little he will divert him.

332: *It is typical of the evil spirit to transform himself into an angel of light, to go in by the devout soul's way but to come out his own way; I mean he introduces sound and pious thoughts, suited to the piety of that soul; but then little by little, he tries to achieve his own purposes, by dragging the soul down to his secret designs and corrupt purposes.*

For example, take the case of a zealous priest: "You are wasting too much time contemplating; souls are waiting for you." And he ends up neglecting his mental prayer.

Or, perhaps, during meditation, the devil will come to a priest with a poetical inclination and inspire him with beautiful canticles to the Blessed Virgin Mary, thereby distracting him from the meditation he should be making. To the mathematician, he would not suggest rhymes, but dazzling problems that would make Einstein grow pale. For an apostle, he will suggest fantastic conferences that would convert people en masse.

The devil succeeded in fooling the Curé of Ars on three occasions. What would you have done if you had wanted to ensnare the Curé? Probably, you would have sent him a woman of ill repute. Yet, the Curé of Ars would have converted her and would not have sinned. The devil is more subtle. He scrutinized the virtues of the Curé, his hatred of sin, his love for penance, his love for prayer, and that is what he came up with:

: Go to a Trappist monastery to mourn over your sins, to perform long and hard penances, to enjoy a contemplative life!

The Curé of Ars fell for it, and not once, but at least twice.

FIFTH RULE No. 333

THIS IS THE GOLDEN RULE,
WHICH WILL ENABLE US TO DISCOVER THE DEVIL'S TAIL.

333: *We should pay great attention to the entire train of thought. If the beginning, middle and end are wholly sound, tending to what is completely innocent, this is a sign of the good angel; but the train of thought suggested sometimes leads to something that is bad or at least distracting, or less good than what the soul had originally proposed to do; sometimes it undermines our strength of mind or disturbs us by destroying our peace and tranquility of mind and the unperturbed condition already obtained: these are clear signs that the thoughts come from the evil spirit, the enemy of our progress and everlasting salvation.*

You cannot have a vague notion of things. If the intention and the aim are visibly good, one must not immediately conclude that it is from God. It could still come from the devil, especially if it involves a grace which is apparently miraculous. The devil may utilize all his cunning to make us fall... and in two ways: either by making one believe that a certain mysterious phenomenon comes from God, and thereby gradually leading courageous souls to discouragement or error; or, by trying to discredit a true action of God, a true saint, with God's permission.

This delicate but safe rule is based on the moral principle: *"Bonum ex integra causa, malum ex quocumque defectu."* In order for something to merit the adjective **good**, it must be perfectly good; for it to be evil, it suffices that the slightest thing be bad. For example, if in a very good cake or an excellent wine, one adds an ounce of strychnine or a few drops of gasoline, it can no longer be called good. For something to be called bad it suffices that the smallest thing be bad: for example, a good soup which is burnt, or a beautiful, silk dress on which some drops of oil have fallen.

This exquisite Bordeaux wine if put into an empty gas can, would be disaster. Listen to what St. Ignatius says: *"If the beginning and middle are good one can still not decide, unless the end is good also. BEWARE!"* And St. Ignatius is explicit in order that we may not be deceived: "If everything is good, then it is from God." But if anything bad happens in the course of events, it cannot be from God. For example, the parish priest I mentioned earlier. One of the youth became a Communist, and others stopped going to Communion. The advice of "apostolate of exercise" in dancing halls with the best of intentions is bad or, at least, dissipating (the youth acquire a taste for dancing); or, it is **less good** than what used to be done (the youth stop communicating).

St. Ignatius explains now those signs which are more difficult to grasp. If a certain thought weakens our soul, troubles it, makes it uneasy, takes away the peace which it had before, then it is a clear sign that this thought comes from the devil.

At Paris, St. Ignatius had this thought: "If you want to found an order that will influence the ruling class in the midst of a humanistic century, you have to work at becoming a distinguished Latinist." So far, so good. "Therefore, you must also buy and read the works of Erasmus, so universally praised." He needed, at all costs, to read his book. Thus, St. Ignatius bought the book *Miles Christi.* Every day he read a few pages. It was truly beautiful Latin... but after a while, St. Ignatius realized that after each reading of Erasmus, he had no longer the fervor and compunction he usually had. He had it cross-checked and ended by renouncing Erasmus. It was only years later that the Church realized the damage this humanist writer had caused to the youth, and the book was condemned. Ignatius had understood this only when he lost his recollection. Earlier we said something about Magdalen of the Cross, who, at the beginning of the century of St. Theresa of Avila, fooled almost the whole of Spain. She, while levitating, received the host, which detached itself from the hand of the priest and flew through the air before resting upon her tongue. On certain days she had either the stigmata or the sweats of blood, and she announced the defeat and imprisonment of Francis I by the Spanish army at Pavia (they did not have telecommunications in those days). Hence, the tide of enthusiasm of which she was the cause. Common people, parish priests, bishops, emperors, many venerated her and consulted with her.

However, an apostolic visitor sent by Rome was shocked by some details he saw in her convent. He spoke to each of the sisters and, especially, with the Mother Abbess, Magdalen of the Cross, who, eventually, confessed that, while a young shepherdess, she had sold her soul to the devil in return for his giving her the power of performing prodigies. Thus, she deceived everybody for thirty years. Notice, however, that the pseudo-miracles were only prodigies relative to us. The devil could quite easily transport a host from the ciborium to a communicant, bring news from Pavia to Cordova, in the twinkling of an eye... or raise someone from the ground, or make them bleed.

The same thing happened in Paris a few years later. A house-maid called Nicole Tavernier performed prodigies. The host came to her all by itself; she knew what was happening miles away. From Paris, she found herself transported to Tours, and, within two hours, she was back in Paris. The whole of Paris was talking about her, and she was audacious enough to order the bishop of Paris to hold a public procession (in which the French Parliament took part). Next to her, a true saint, Madame Accarie (later to become the Blessed Mary of the Incarnation, Carmelite) said: "No, this is not from God!" She was right. Nicole finished lamentably and became a Huguenot. Madame Accarie surprised her in her flagrant telling of lies and vain actions. That was sufficient evidence.

In the same century there was, in Rome, a religious who was called holy and performed prodigies. Cardinals disagreed over the origin of these extraordinary events. They asked St. Philip Neri to go and see.

Philip went to the convent, rang the bell and demanded brutally:

: Excuse me, I have come to see the saint.

: It is I!

This was sufficient. Philip left, convinced as to the 'sanctity' of the 'holy' religious and the origins of her prodigies.

Therefore, BEWARE!

Fr. Ibanes, a Dominican, in his study on St. Theresa of Avila said: "These graces, 'gratis datæ' of visions and revelations are given for the sanctification of the neighbor. If, instead of bringing fruits of sanctity, these graces rendered them rather disobedient, proud, anti-establishment, etc., it would be a sign that these miraculous facts do not come from God."

"You know a tree by its fruits." Even then, watch out! Look closely into it.

A monk came to see me once saying that he wanted to enter a Carthusian monastery. He had even asked permission from his abbot, but he had not spoken to his confessor about it. This was an evident sign that it was the devil who wanted him in the Carthusian monastery: his not having spoken to his confessor until all had been arranged.

SIXTH RULE No. 334

334: *When the enemy of mankind is perceived and known by his serpent's tail, the evil conclusion to which he leads men, the person so tempted will find it useful afterwards to retrace the course of his thoughts, beginning with the good ideas originally suggested and the way in which he was gradually brought down from the heights of spiritual satisfaction and joy to accept the other's corrupt purpose. The understanding and noting of this experience will help him to be on his guard in future against the enemy's usual tricks.*

This is why self-examination is necessary. St. Bernard said to his monks: "Examine each of your actions." St. Ignatius tells us: "by the serpent's tail"... The snake, you see, hides under the leaves in order not to be seen. But if someone suspects he is there he will look carefully. The snake is cunning enough to hide, but it does not pay close attention to its tail, still visible. You can recognize him by his tail and, thus, defeat him. Likewise, it will happen that you fall into the devil's trap, yet do not be afraid. It may take a while before you realize that you have been caught. Make an attentive examination: how did the devil catch you? At the beginning... perhaps at a moment of fatigue, or perhaps when enthusiastic, or not feeling well. What did he suggest to the Curé of Ars? The horror of sin, a contemplative life: he minimized the ordinary work of the parish priest. Check thoroughly the sophisms by which he catches you, see the mistakes you made. Perhaps you abandoned your meditation or your spiritual reading, you waste time reading the newspaper, magazines... Perhaps you neglected your examination of conscience, you received a serious warning which you discarded as if not worth the bother. You did not reveal to your spiritual director a particular relationship, or an imprudence. Little by little, the devil will make you lose your first fervor. You will gain much experience, and knowledge of self, if you examine the method used by the devil to catch you. Generally, he repeats himself and comes back with the same allurements. Take note, examine the development of the good ideas: in this there is a precious method of examination.

SEVENTH RULE No. 335

335: *When souls are advancing from good to better, the touch of the good angel is soft, light and gentle, like a drop of water making its way into a sponge. The touch of the evil spirit is rough, accompanied by noise and disturbance, like a drop of water falling on stone. But their action is the opposite with those who are going from bad to worse. The reason is that the state of soul is either contrary or similar to these angels. When it is contrary they make their way in with perceptible noise and sensation; when it's similar they come in quietly, like a man coming into his own house when the door is open.*

This rule is very useful and may bring great lights, not only for individual combat but also for the general battle of the two standards. Sarda y Salvani, in his book *Liberalism is a Sin,* quotes St. Ignatius' seventh rule to clarify one's judgment of ambiguous events: he shows this very clearly in the events over which we are badly informed. It is based on this principle: one is shocked by contrary principles or ideas, whereas thoughts which go along with our way of thinking appear good and natural, as if normal. For example, a progressive priest reads an encyclical that reminds him of the principles of the Faith. He is shocked by it. "With this pope, theology cannot advance, etc." Contrariwise, if he reads an 'advanced,' Modernist article, which flatters revolutionary priests, he approves of it, "This is good, by it one will deepen his wisdom." Often, we see simple peasants, good retreatants, with articles in their hands which have shocked them. They do not see the astuteness, but since it is a progressive article, it was sufficient to shock them. Likewise, they hear us preach on hell during the retreat, and, knowing the good impact it has on sinners, they instructively nod their heads as a sign of agreement. They know very clearly what is influencing the first priest, and what is influencing the others.

Likewise, one hears talk of a new movement which has sprung-up: for example, The Moral Rearmament, or a new political party. People speak wonders about them, but what do they say exactly? Who says it? Who are the leaders? Where are the supernatural fruits of humility, faith, obedience? What do worldly people think of it? What do men of God think of it? Thus, without having studied these movements, one would find out whether they come from God or from the devil. This can give much enlightenment concerning movements you know little about. Just as the Holy Ghost promotes peace, spiritual joy, charity, chastity, meekness, humility, etc., likewise, that which promotes the contrary does not come from Him. A young, Chinese virgin, who is a Catholic, will have the same reaction as the virgins of the first centuries. Also, the impious materialists (Communists, Nazis) have a reaction similar to Nero and Diocletian towards the doctrine of Christ and the Church. And these that are more or less taken in by error (i.e. the liberal Catholics) approve them. In the same way, the sedevacantists, who call the pope a heretic, cannot be inspired by the spirit of God, even if they are very pious, say nice things and perform miracles!

EIGHTH RULE No. 336

Beware! Even when the beginning is from God, the rest may be infiltrated by the devil. The devil is able to imitate true apparitions: for example, St. Ignatius' famous vision of the Blessed Trinity at Manresa. In the same place, a few days later, Our Lord appeared. St. Ignatius was surprised, troubled, and he wondered why Our Lord looked the way He did. He made the sign of the Cross and, all of a sudden, the apparition was transformed into a serpent that disappeared, leaving behind a nauseating odor. A person could very well have an extraordinary mystical grace from Our Lord, and then allow himself to be fooled by the devil: "This very night, before the cock crows twice, you will deny Me thrice." And St. Peter, who had already received extraordinary, mystical favors, let himself be deceived by the devil. Yes, the great Peter of Cana, of the miraculous draught of fish, who had said *"You are Christ, Son of the Living God!"* Gentlemen, **BEWARE!**

336: *When the consolation has no preceding occasion, whilst it is true that this cannot be illusory, since it can come only from God Our Lord, as we have said, you, the spiritual recipient, must scrutinize the process with great care. You must distinguish exactly the specific time or the actual consolation from the subsequent stage when the soul is glowing from the favor conferred upon it, a sort of afterglow from the consolation which is now over. In this second stage the soul often makes different resolutions and plans which are not the direct result of the action of God Our Lord. They may be due to the soul's own activity, based on established habits of mind or the implications of ideas or judgments previously formed; they may be the result of the action of the good or the evil spirit. So they have to be very carefully scrutinized before we can give them complete credit and put them into effect.*

Beware! All ascetical phenomena, and all the more so, the mystical ones, must be examined with the greatest care. Especially in the case of revelations or visions, one must carefully distinguish that which certainly is of God from the reactions, reasonings, and conclusions which are subsequent to God's work, and which come either from the seer, or from witnesses or examiners, or especially, from the enthusiastic, who are perhaps too excited over it.

This is why, in the presence of visions or private revelations of divine origin, one must remember the words of St. Peter after his allusion to the Transfiguration: *"Sed habemus firmiorem propheticum sermonem."* But we have words which are more sure, those of the prophets," those of Revelation; that is, those of the official Church. Humility: *"vigilate et orate, ne intretis in tentationem," "spiritus probate..."* "Watch and pray, that you enter not into temptation," **"Test the spirits..."** So says St. Ignatius.

"By their fruits you shall know them. Do men gather grapes of thorns or figs of thistles?" (Mt. 7:16). Invoke Our Lady of Good Counsel, and imitate above all the Virgin, most prudent, who asked the archangel Gabriel: "How shall this be, since I know not man?" One can see that she was used to being tempted under the appearance of good, but this Spouse of the Holy Ghost acted with prudence. Invoke St. Joseph, watchful guardian of the Universal Church. Invoke the great archangels St. Michael, St. Gabriel, St. Raphael, and all the heavenly spirits who watch over us and our institutions.

FATHER IBANES, O.P.
A Report on the Subject of St. Theresa of Avila.

Permit me to add here the important report of a learned Dominican theologian, who lived in the time of St. Theresa. He alone (perhaps with one other) took to the defense of St. Theresa. All the great theologians of Avila agreed in their conclusion that the devil had fooled Theresa of Avila. It was he who gave the rules to determine whether Theresa was being led by the devil or by the spirit of God. He concluded victoriously that the Spirit of God was leading her. He died two years later. St. Theresa, who had been greatly encouraged by him to work on the reform of the Carmel, saw him enter Heaven without having to pass through purgatory.

These rules do not apply to the discernments of the first week. They relate to those which St. Ignatius lists for the second week: namely, rules for superior cases, especially for mystics.

Fr. Ibanes, O.P. was a professor of theology at Avila. St. Theresa consulted him on the project of the reform of the Carmel. She praised him in her autobiography in chapters 9 and 33.

He gave his report proving, before the competent judges, that Theresa was guided by God. It happened twenty years before Theresa's death. It is perhaps the most important favor of the sanctity of the Carmelite reformer. It will give assistance to those who have questions about recent visions, some certainly false, and others certainly true, while some may remain doubtful.

I will quote from Fr. Ibanes:

: *How does one know who truly has visions and revelations from God?*

: *How does one discover that somebody is deceived, either ourselves or others?*

At home, Theresa, as a child, heard voices from Heaven, concerning both the immense joys reserved for the good and the terrible torments awaiting the wicked. She heard of the martyrs' lives, and so she had a desire to go to the Moors. At the age of 19, the example of a holy religious inspired her to enter the Carmel of the Incarnation. She entered at the age of 21, filled with good desires mixed with many obstacles. She did not apply herself fully to mental prayer. Her friendships and familiarities with those who were not wholly given over to God were a tremendous obstacle for her spiritual advancement, and even for her salvation. One day, she finally applied herself with renewed ardor to the exercise of mental prayer, with much penance and fasting, as well as to complete obedience to her confessor. She was blessed with many special favors. She believed that Our Lord spoke to her, teaching her hidden mysteries, future events concerning heresies that were ravaging France, and certain projects she was to perform later on. She greatly feared being fooled by the devil on account of her sins.

The example of Magdalen of the Cross who, a few years previous, had been the talk of the whole of Spain, was still fresh in the minds of confessors who feared that Theresa was equally fooled by the devil. Magdalen of the Cross, while a young shepherdess, had sold her soul to the devil on condition that she would perform prodigies, and for thirty years she did just that. Everybody went to see her: the clergy, the emperor, the common people. She even announced at Cordova that the King of France, Francis I, in 1525 had been defeated and taken prisoner by the Spanish at Pavia. Everybody was saying, "What a great saint!" Slowly, however the trappings of the devil were discovered, and people understood that she, indeed, performed prodigies, not miracles.

Fr. Ibanes brings up the objection that, often, learned doctors have been deceived. Saints maintain that very few visions are true... If the visions are true, they are miraculous, but miracles do not happen without a grave necessity, and there is no such need to confirm the Faith in the cloister. The saints dislike very much that their particular favors from God be made public; they prefer to hide them away.

The famous Gerson, at the time of the Council of Constance, affirmed that St. Catherine of Siena could not have had such a familiarity with God. He wrote against her and demanded that the council silence her and even condemn her... We have never read of anyone who has advanced in the love of God without being contradicted and without people wanting to destroy his reputation. Some just decide against the truth.

* * * * *

Therefore, although this servant of God is an object of contradiction, it is no reason for a prudent man to deem as illusory favors received from above. This is especially true given that those who persist in their erroneous manner had never spoken to Theresa but, in fact, had formed an opinion from second hand testimonies. Certain things may seem bad, but if circumstances are taken into account, they become very holy and virtuous. For example, to take someone else's property is evil, but to do so for the advantage of the proprietor (i.e. to prevent him from killing himself) is virtuous. In the same way, to believe visions too easily is neither wise, nor prudent, but in a given, particular case it can be justified. There is, also, not a single epoch when Our Lord has not had great intimacy with certain souls, from Abraham on. That is why, for as long as the world lasts, God will not lack prophets or friends in His Church. He gives His friendship to those who prepare themselves for it, at every epoch. God makes saints for the good of His Church, for the utility of His Church, and to appease the divine wrath. These necessities exist today!

* * * * *

Thus, we must beware of taking offence when a saint is pointed out by those who know him and have dealt with him. When in doubt as to whether the revelation is truly from God, *one has a very strong proof that it is true and comes from God if one knows that the visionary lives a life of serious Christian perfection.*

It is difficult to give precisions for particular cases in the science of the discernment of spirits. Many of those who possessed this science have been deceived. For example, Gerson, who did much in this area, was sceptical in his approach to the visions of St. Catherine of Siena, because he was ignorant of much of her case, and because God works many things in saints which surpass natural reason.

Examine the effects and the fruits. Just as a doctor sees in the results the invisible evil, so the health of the soul is recognized by its works and the beauty of its life.

"A fructibus eorum cognoscetis eos," said Jesus. "You will recognize them by their fruits" (Mt. 8:16).

These revelations or visions are either good and true (they come from God) or bad and full of lies (they come from the devil). In doubtful cases one will recognize if it comes from God, if it has God's seal upon it. Likewise, if one finds the cunning and craftiness of the devil, then it surely comes from the evil one.

Here are some rules to follow in order to be able to make a good discernment:

1. When the person who has been favored with revelations despises himself and acknowledges his faults during and after the revelations, it is a sign that they come from God.

This sign was found amongst all the servants of God and was missing from the 'mystics' fooled by the devil. On the one hand, humility and love; one the other, pride and trouble. Remember the Blessed Virgin Mary and St. Elizabeth.

2. If the person who has received revelations is afterwards led to interior recollection and to detachment from everything, if he flees the world, thinks nothing of it and despises it thoroughly, then it is an evident sign that what he has received is from God. But if this revelation promotes a spirit of independence, of pride and vanity to the point of boasting about the favors received, it is certainly an illusion.

The spirit of God produces love and true humility. It hates vanity and glamor and despises the world. "My secret is my own," said Isaias.

3. See whether it is a soul of prayer or not, and if in its dealings with others one can see a love of God which is true and not superficial. Never will the soul given over to prayer and who perseveres in it be fooled by the devil, who rather urges her to abandon prayer.

4. See whether he takes great care to consult men of doctrine. See especially whether he hides anything from his confessor. It is a certain sign that there is no illusion if he

follows his confessor's advice. God will not abandon those who have good intentions. The seer who opens up his soul makes an act of humility. That is why, when he does not want to speak to someone learned in these questions, and who will not approve without cross-examination—if the seer cares little about finding out the truth—then one must believe that it is an illusion from the devil. God increases humility when he comes into our souls. To reveal our temptations and our trials is a powerful means of overcoming the devil.

5. Take heed of the advice of people who know the favored soul, and also of the advice of his confessors, who know his conscience. The help of theology alone is not sufficient, especially if we do not have experience, and if the confessors consulted are not in agreement.

6. If he is opposed and contradicted without having done anything to cause it, if the opponents are decent, zealous people, and if, in spite of this, the favored person remains patient, it is God who dwells in his heart, and not the devil deceiving him. Just look at Job...

7. Another proof (which applies only to confessors and spiritual directors) is to see if the soul possesses a great purity of conscience and deep virtue. This is a sure and efficacious way of detecting illusions, because God's favors are for those who keep their soul pure and free from sin.

   "Beati mundo corde," "Blessed are the pure of heart!"

8. Inquire into the spiritual profit of those who treat familiarly with the visionary, because the *"gratis datae"* are gifts for the neighbor. See whether all those in contact with him are God-fearing persons. If, on the contrary, the results are independence, pride, luxury, the "favors" do not come from God, but rather, from the devil, who has transformed himself into an "angel of light."

9. Inquire into what is said and revealed. If he does not want to tell everything to the men of doctrine, if he treats them as ignoramuses, or if he says useless and worldly things which are in no way edifying, one can then be sure that the devil moves him. If, however, he tells everything with great simplicity, and without conceit, to those who are able to judge and understand him, and if the entire thing is decent and in conformity with the teaching of the Church, it comes from God.

10. If, after close examination, one finds nothing blameworthy in the company he keeps and in his conversation, and if he also manifests a profound virtue, then there is evident reason to believe that it is from God. When everybody, and, particularly, the men of doctrine, UNANIMOUSLY approve of him, the origin is certainly divine.

11. Take into account the attitude of the devil towards him. If he approves and manifests his satisfaction, it is a bad sign; if he persecutes him, it is a good sign. To good souls he shows himself horrible; his friends, who are deluded, he leaves in peace.

No doubt, in the beginning it is difficult to recognize clearly if it is from God, but, with time, one will manage.

In St. Theresa's case, she thought only of God and occupied herself wholly with Him. She directed all the glory to God and to the spiritual welfare of souls. For nothing in the world would she have committed even a venial sin. Her whole ambition was to perfect herself and to grow in virtue each day.

She said one day to God:

: Lord, is there no one else among the learned who is more worthy of Your apparitions?

God responded:

: Since those learned in doctrine are not disposed to deal

with Me, I come, as a rejected beggar to find a poor little woman in whom I may find rest and with whom I may correspond.

Jesus also said to her:

: The devil can in no wise give such a contentment, such an interior joy, such a spiritual joy. Neither is he able to produce such love and progress in virtue (a quote of St. Theresa).

Fr. Ibanes in his report on St. Theresa continues:

1. There has never been anyone fooled by the devil who had as many proofs and reasons to believe that what she had received came really from God.

2. The saints have not taught that we must not receive some revelations or look upon some persons as holy. What they have taught is that we must not place faith too easily in them. When dealing with things so elevated one must not believe too easily.

3. His Majesty, desiring to console His faithful servants and, through them, to save other souls, has always had the custom of granting extraordinary favors to certain persons. But there are *a thousand reasons to believe this religious, favored by God, and there is no reason to disbelieve her.*

4. In the beginning she exposed her favors only to confessors and to those who could enlighten her, with the recommendation that they keep it secret.

5. Fr. Ibanes assisted at the cure of a kidney patient for whom St. Theresa prayed. At another time, Our Lord appeared to her, showing her His wounded side, and saying that He would refuse her nothing which she would ask. A benefactor who had lost his sight immediately recovered it. She worked numerous other bodily cures.

These pages are a résumé of the report made by Fr. Ibanes. Please excuse me for not having cited it in its integrity. Herein one finds what is essential for discerning the divine or diabolical origin of mystical charisms in a soul.

L-M. Barrielle, CP.CR.V.

Make Use of the Spiritual Exercises Given to Saint Ignatius by Mary.

"... St. Ignatius learned from the Mother of God herself how he should fight the combats of Our Lord."

"It is from her hands that he received this most perfect code... of which the soldier of Christ must make use..."

POPE PIUS XI

THIS IS A PROVISIONAL AND PRIVATE PUBLICATION CONFORMING TO THE DECREES OF POPE URBAN VIII. THE AUTHOR DECLARES THAT HE WILL SUBMIT TO ALL THE DECISIONS OF THE HOLY ROMAN CHURCH.

If you wish to make a five-day Ignatian Retreat, from which the contents of this book have been taken, you may contact one of the following retreat houses:

St. Ignatius Retreat House
209 Tackora Trail
Ridgefield, Connecticut 06877
(203) 431-0201

St. Aloysius Retreat Center
19101 Bear Creek Road
Los Gatos, California 95030-9519
(408) 354-7703

Our Lady of Sorrows Retreat House
750 East Baseline Road
Phoenix, Arizona 85040-6613
(602) 268-7673

For additional copies of this book and a free catalog of Angelus Press publications contact:

ANGELUS PRESS
2915 Forest Avenue, Kansas City, Missouri 64109
(816) 753-3150 FAX (816) 753-3557